9-03-09

Note to Reader:
The fact that this volume is included in our library or classroom does not mean that ~~Calvary Churches~~ CCS endorses all of its contents. A well-rounded education is based upon Biblical truths. It is always our goal to use worthwhile publications in this process. Some source material, however, may serve broader educational purposes without necessarily reflecting, in full or in part, Calvary's well-known positions on important topics. Please direct concerns to the appropriate office.

THIS IS A FREE BOOK
-- not for resale --
Embrace Books
www.embracebooks.org

Grasslands

by Elizabeth Ring • Photographs by Dwight Kuhn

BLACKBIRCH PRESS
An imprint of Thomson Gale, a part of The Thomson Corporation

Detroit • New York • San Francisco • San Diego • New Haven, Conn. • Waterville, Maine • London • Munich

© 2005 Thomson Gale, a part of the Thomson Corporation.

Thomson and Star Logo are trademarks and Gale and Blackbirch Press are registered trademarks used herein under license.

For more information, contact
The Gale Group, Inc.
27500 Drake Rd.
Farmington Hills, MI 48331-3535
Or you can visit our Internet site at http://www.gale.com

ALL RIGHTS RESERVED
No part of this work covered by the copyright hereon may be reproduced or used in any form or by any means—graphic, electronic, or mechanical, including photocopying, recording, taping, Web distribution or information storage retrieval systems—without the written permission of the publisher.

Every effort has been made to trace the owners of copyrighted material.

Photo Credits: Cover, all photos © Dwight Kuhn Photography except pp. 32-33 © W. Perry Conway/CORBIS and p. 22 © Corel

---

LIBRARY OF CONGRESS CATALOGING-IN-PUBLICATION DATA

Ring, Elizabeth, 1920-
  Grasslands / by Elizabeth Ring.
      p. cm. — (Communities in nature)
  Includes bibliographical references and index.
  ISBN 1-4103-0318-7 (hard cover : alk. paper)
  1. Grasslands—Juvenile literature. I. Title II. Series: Ring, Elizabeth, 1920- . Communities in nature.

QH87.7.R56 2005
578.74—dc22   2004013976

Printed in China
10 9 8 7 6 5 4 3 2 1

Introduction

In meadows and prairies, grass covers acres of ground. Grasslands look as if nothing grows there but grass. You listen for sounds of things you can't see. You hear tiny hums, soft rustlings, little chirps. Somewhere, beneath the feathery grass tips, something's alive. You're not all alone in this grass-covered place.

Grasslands cover acres of land where meadow and prairie creatures live.

In the Meadow

I love the meadow any time of the year, but I think I like summer the best. Butterflies flit slowly from flower to flower and the flowers nod their bright heads. At the edge of the woods, steamy mists rise. It's cooler there under the trees. In the meadow, there's hardly a tree to give shade. I don't care. I breathe in hot, weedy smells and I ramble around—as lazily as the butterflies fly.

A warm, quiet, flowery meadow invites visitors all summer long.

But the spring is fine, too. That's when the round yellow dandelions are all over the grass. Then, when the yellow petals dry up, white fluffy balls show up in their place. You can blow on the fluff and watch it spin off—like tiny white parachutes tossing around in the air.

Yellow dandelions turn into white fluff that floats off into the air when you blow it away.

Lots of meadow flowers are named for other things—like oxeye daisies that look like an ox's eyes. Coltsfoot leaves are supposed to look like a young horse's small feet. Whatever their names, I just like to look at all the yellow, orange, purple, red, blue, and white flowers all over the meadow—like crayons stuck in a big green box. That's how the whole field looks to me.

Left: Flowering plants fill the meadow with purple, yellow, orange and white blooms.

Right: Grasshoppers jump high over the meadow grass.

All sorts of small creatures live deep in the meadow grass. Grasshoppers are down there, chewing on leaves. Every once in a while, you hear one sing a scratchy song or you see one jump straight up from the grass. If I could jump as far as a grasshopper can jump, I'd get to school really fast. I don't try to catch grasshoppers of any kind. Some spit a brown juice that can smear up your hands.

Crab spiders don't hop. They walk sideways, fast, the way crabs crawl around on the shore. What these spiders do, too, is hide underneath flowers and snatch visiting flies, wasps and bees. You would think a big bee could easily escape from a spider so small. But the spider's four long front legs are strong and act just like a trap.

A crab spider captures a bee that comes to a flower to sip nectar.

A garter snake coils itself up on the ground, sunning itself.

One day, I almost stepped on a garter snake in the field. Its tongue was flicking in and out and it was looking at me with its big, bulgy eye. I jumped away. But then I found out that garter snakes aren't poisonous and won't hurt you at all. In fact, people like to have them in their gardens because they eat mice and other animals that chew up garden plants. Now I know that a snake with three orange or yellow rows of dots down its back is my friend.

When I see a woodchuck sitting straight up in the meadow, looking scared, I stand still. I don't want it to run into its den. I'd like to look into its burrow myself, though, sometime. I've heard the den is a long tunnel with rooms off to the sides. That's where woodchuck babies are born. And that's where the woodchuck hibernates, sleeping all winter long.

A woodchuck stretches high to see what is going on in the meadow grass nearby.

A red fox would like a woodchuck to eat—or a mouse, or a rabbit, frog, lizard, or almost any animal it can catch. It's not a picky eater at all. It loves corn, berries, and apples. It even eats birds. Foxes have perky ears and sharp noses and eyes. A fox is a lot like my dog—the same shape and size. They both bark. They are, in fact, related, but my dog is not a wild animal and never has to hunt for his lunch. He gets it right out of his dish.

A red fox cocks its head toward a sound that might be a rabbit to chase.

I hope the fox won't find the killdeer bird's nest I saw yesterday. It's hardly a nest. It has no sides. The speckled eggs lay right on the ground and looked just like stones. And a bird parent was protecting the eggs. When the eggs hatch, the chicks look like baby chickens and ducks, fluffy and wide awake. They aren't naked and blind the way most other baby birds are. I like the killdeer's loud call—*kill-deer*—as if the bird is laughing out loud as it says its own name. (The bird won't kill any deer, of course!)

A killdeer protects the spotted eggs she has laid on the ground—not in a nest.

A Savannah sparrow's call is more chirpy—a high, soft *chip-chip-chip* and a long, buzzy sound—like *tsip-tsp-tsp se-e-e-srr*. This bird hides its nest under the grass. The nest looks like a cup and is lined with soft grass. It's a bit safer place, I'd say, than what the killdeer chicks have.

A Savannah sparrow lifts its head to sing its high, chirpy song.

Male goldfinches show off their gold and black feathers and sing like canaries.

A goldfinch doesn't chirp like a sparrow, and it doesn't have a killdeer-like cry. It sings more like a canary—in musical trills. The male goldfinch looks as bright as he sounds. He is golden-colored and black. His mate is not so splashy. Her feathers are greenish brown. Goldfinches like thistle seeds to eat. We always add thistle to our bird feeders at home. It brings goldfinches to our backyard.

The day I saw a kestrel, it was sitting still on a tree stump, staring at the ground. I knew it wasn't looking for seeds. A kestrel is a kind of hawk, and all hawks eat meat. If it spots a mouse, a grasshopper, a snake, an insect, or a bird, it will dive, feet first, and grab its prey with its claws. When kestrels fly over the field, they hardly flap their wings. They swoop on the air—silently—looking for something to dive on from up there.

Kestrels are swift, fierce hunters that grab their prey with sharp claws.

Butterflies land feetfirst, too, when they feed. But the flowers they light on aren't hurt at all. The butterflies have no beaks or claws. They drift from one flower to another and settle softly to eat. They don't even have mouths—only long tubes they dip into a flower to sip sweet nectar juice. A tiger swallowtail butterfly has the same yellow and black colors a tiger has. And its tail is shaped like a swallow bird's tail. That's how it gets its two names.

Tiger swallowtail butterflies wear tiger colors and have tails shaped like a swallow's.

My friend takes his butterfly net to the field. He's good at catching butterflies and moths, without hurting them. Sometimes, he pops his net on top of one. Sometimes he swishes his net sideways through the air. Then he peels back the soft net to get a good look at his catch. Lots of moths and butterflies look alike. My friend carries a little book that tells which is which. He always lets his butterflies go. As it is, they have very short lives to live.

We both think all the wildlife should get to be in the meadow as long as they can. We, ourselves, always wait until the last minute to leave.

You can catch all kinds of flying insects when you carry a soft butterfly net.

In the Tallgrass Prairie

Out on the tallgrass prairie, the tops of some of the grasses reach high over my head. That can make me feel very small. That's all right. Almost every animal that lives here is smaller that I. They hide, but even if I can't see them in the tall grass, I know they're there. I've been here so many times before.

The grass in a tallgrass prairie can reach over your head.

I watched a big golden garden spider for a long time one calm, sunny day. It was hanging head-down in its web. The web was a circle of crossed strings and some zigzag lines. It stretched out wide between two tall, tough stems of grass. All day, that spider sits in the middle of its web, head-down. It waits for some insect to fly into its web and get stuck on the sticky threads. When a bug hits the web, the web shakes, and the spider runs to capture its prey.

Up close, you see that a golden garden spider stands on her head in her spider web.

When a grasshopper gets stuck in the spider's web, the spider gets a really big meal. I saw the spider kill a 'hopper one day—with one bite. Spiders can't chew. Instead, they spit juices that turn their prey's body to mush. The spider sucks the mush up. Spiders can swallow quite a few insects that spoil plants. In fact, we really like spiders to live in our garden at home.

This golden garden spider has captured a grasshopper that got stuck in her web.

Honeybees gather sweet, juicy nectar from flowers and carry it back to the hives.

Honeybees can't chew any better than spiders can. They don't even have a mouth—just a tongue that is sort of a straw. Worker honeybees work all day, sipping nectar from milkweed and other sweet flowers. They buzz busily back and forth, carrying nectar to their hives. The nectar is not just to eat all by themselves. It's also food for the queen bee and other bees that live in the hive. Some of the nectar is stored in honeycomb cells. That nectar becomes the honey that we, ourselves, eat from beehives.

Black-eyed Susans are flowers that honeybees like. I like them, too—to look at, not eat. Their long, yellow petals swoop out around their black, button-like eyes. All summer long, the Susans stand tall, one flower on each long, hairy stem. You hardly ever see Susans drooping their heads. They mostly stare up at the sky.

The sweetness of black-eyed Susans attract many bees and butterflies.

Butterflies visit meadow flowers all summer long, just as bees do. One butterfly is called a great spangled fritillary. A "frit" (for short) has wide orange-and-black wings with lots of speckles and dots. That's why it is called "fritillary"— meaning it has specks. Black-eyed Susans are just one of the sweet flowers the butterflies sip nectar from all day long.

A great spangled butterfly flutters its spotted wings as it visits a black-eyed susan.

Any fly, bee, or butterfly that visits a flower is lucky if it doesn't get caught by an ambush bug. The bug's yellow-green color makes it look part of the plant. It sits still on a plant and waits to grab (ambush) its prey—the way a spider sits and waits in its web. It will grab a bug with its long, thick front legs and poison it with spit from its short beak. Then, like a spider, it sucks its prey dry. The only thing ambush bugs have to worry about is that a bird or mouse might ambush them.

An ambush bug hides among goldenrod petals, waiting to snatch other visiting bugs.

A bobolink perched on a fence post is probably searching for bugs—any kind. An ambush bug would make quite a good snack. What I like best about a male bobolink is his song. It makes you want to sing, too. His notes really sound like *bob-o-link* or *bob-o-lee*. His name fits him just fine.

A bobolink perches on a fence post and looks out over its prairie home.

Sometimes, you come across a yellow-throat warbler's nest, hidden in the tall grass. Both parents feed their chicks, and I can tell the male by his black mask. His tune sounds something like *witchity, witchity, witchity* or *peachity, peachity, peachity*. It's a song that would make anybody cheer up.

A yellow-throat warbler stuffs a small caterpillar into its chick's beak.

Prairie chickens don't sing at all. They cackle and cluck—the way farm chickens do. At mating time, the roosters put in a big show on what's called their "booming ground." Early one morning, I watched five or six roosters stamping their feet and making loud, booming calls. Their necks puffed out to make big orange balls. They flapped their wings at each other, but they didn't get into fights. One rooster found a hen that seemed to like his big act.

Prairie chicken roosters put on a big show on their "booming grounds."

33

The white-tailed deer hardly makes any noise as it roams through the prairie grass. The one I saw one afternoon was a female, a doe. She was grazing in a place where the grass wasn't tall enough to hide her from me. She slowly lifted her head up and twitched her big ears. Then, four or five times, she ducked her head, ate grass, and lifted her head again. It was as if she was playing some little game with me! If she'd been afraid, she'd have stamped her feet, snorted, and leaped away—with her white tail in the air. I was glad she stayed.

An alert-eared white-tailed deer doe lifts her head to see if it's safe to quietly browse.

A cottontail rabbit's big ears tell it when it is time to leap swiftly to safety.

Cottontail rabbits have white fur on the undersides of their tails, just like the deer. You can see the white part when the rabbit runs—if you look quick. A rabbit can run as fast as you can ride a bike. Before the rabbit takes off, it gives a flick to its big ears—as if it's saying "Catch me if you can." All animals have their own ways to talk. My dog tells me he's happy when he wags his tail high.

Meadow voles have the same enemies that rabbits have—snakes, coyotes, hawks, and owls. And, when it's scared, a vole will stamp its hind feet the way a rabbit does. But it can't run as fast as a rabbit can. All it can do is hide in the burrows and long tunnels voles dig. Voles sometimes build their nests underground, and sometimes outside under grass.

Meadow voles dive into their burrows when danger comes near.

37

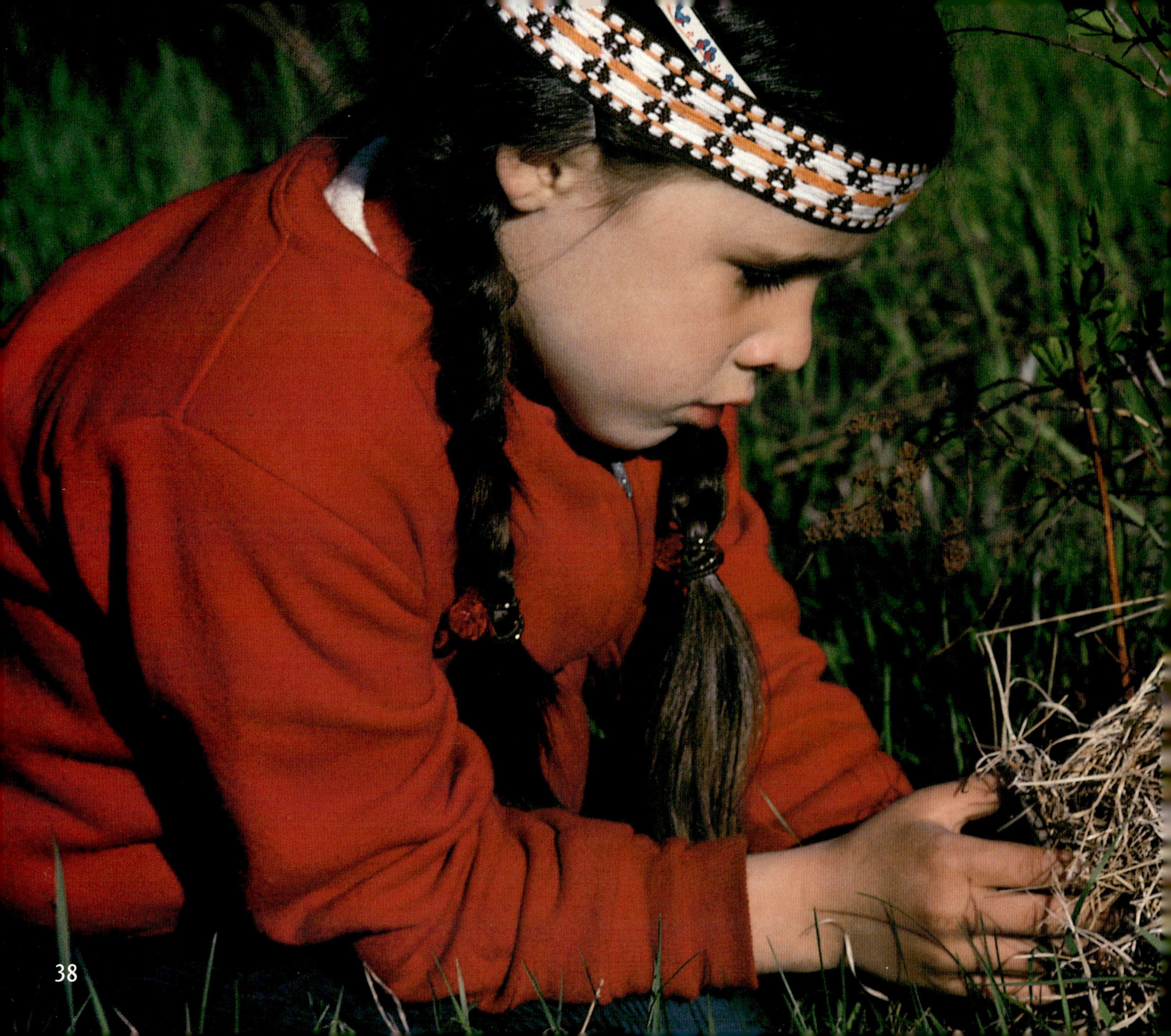

I found a vole nest in the grass one day. It looked like an old ragged ball made of dry grass. The kits had left long ago. Maybe they had moved underground to live in their family den. So many animals use the prairie to hide in, hunt in, make nests in, raise families in! I think the tall grasses are pretty good to them all. For me, the prairie makes a fine place to find out how they all live.

A meadow vole's empty nest looks like an old ball of dried grass.

More About Grasslands

Ambush bug

Ambush bugs are short, wide insects related to assassin bugs and stinkbugs. Their strong claws can hold onto insects twice an ambush bug's size.

American goldfinches fly by flapping their wings to rise, coasting in a slight fall, then rising again—like a roller-coaster ride.

American kestrels are also called "sparrow hawks." They do not look like sparrows, but are smaller than other birds in the hawk family.

Black and yellow **garden spiders** have big bellies and long, hairy legs with yellow and black bands. Male garden spiders make their webs on the outer part of the female's web.

Black-eyed Susans are yellow-flowered, hairy-leaved plants in the coneflower family. Each stalk has one 2 to 3-inch (5 to 8 cm) flower.

Bobolinks are songbirds related to blackbirds and orioles. Male bobolinks have yellow and white feathers in summer and tan ones in winter. Females are tan all year long.

Bobolink

Crab spider

Cottontail rabbits have long ears and webbed toes on their hind legs. Like deer, female rabbits are called does and male rabbits are called bucks.

Crab spiders are small spiders that do not spin webs to catch insects. They lie in wait to ambush their prey. Their first four legs are curved and look like a crab's claws.

Dandelions in bloom have yellow flowers. Because of their toothy leaves, French people called a dandelion *dent de lion* ("lion's tooth").

Garter snakes are small, slim reptiles. They feed on tadpoles and young frogs, small salamanders, fish, and snails.

Grasslands are open, sunny places where there are few trees and many kinds of grasses and wildflowers.

Great spangled fritillaries fly higher off the ground than most butterflies. They like to feed on tall plants, such as black-eyed Susans, thistle, and milkweed.

Greater prairie chickens are roosters and hens with black and tan feathers. So few chickens live on prairies today, that they are on an endangered species list in some states.

Honeybees are called social bees. They live together in a beehive (or honeycomb). Each hive has many small wax cells

Great spangled fritillary

43

Killdeer

in which young bees are raised and nectar is stored.

Killdeer are part of a bird family called plovers. Most plovers live by the sea, but killdeer live far from the water. They feed mostly on insects.

Meadows are fields where many kinds of grasses grow 2 to 3 feet (60 to 90 cm) high in temperate (mild) climates.

Meadow voles are small, gray-furred, mouse-like animals. They are preyed on by many animals, but many voles live for one or two years.

Red foxes are bushy-tailed members of the canine (dog) family. A male fox is called a reynard, and the female is called a vixen. Young foxes are called pups or kits.

Savannah sparrows are small, brown and white streaked birds with yellowish eye rings. The sparrows are named for Savannah, Georgia, where they were discovered.

Short-horned grasshoppers hop in grassy places. Their two "horns" are antennae (feelers) on their heads. Males "sing" by rubbing their back legs against their front wings.

Tallgrass prairies are places where switchgrass, Indian grass, bluestem, and many other grasses grow from 5 to 8 feet (1.5 to 2.5 m) tall.

Short-horned grasshopper

Yellow-throat warbler

Tiger swallowtail butterflies are large butterflies called "tiger" for their orange and black colors. They are called "swallowtail" for their long, pointed tails that look like swallow birds' tails.

White-tailed deer males are called bucks, stags, or harts. Females are called does or hinds. These deer can run up to 40 miles (6.4 km) an hour and jump 9 feet (270 cm) high.

Yellow-throat warblers are perky, wren-like birds with yellow throats and small, upturned tails. They warble their songs.

For More Information

Butterfield, Moira. *Animals on Plains and Prairies*. Oxford, England: Raintree, 1999.
Dvorak, David. *Sea of Grass*. New York: Simon & Schuster, 1994.
Murray, Peter. *Prairies*. Chanhassen, MN: Child's World, 1996.
Paul, Tessa. *In Fields and Meadows*. New York: Crabtree, 1997.
Pipes, Rose. *Grasslands*. Oxford, England: Raintree, 1998.

http://mbgnet.mobot.or/sets/grasslnd/index.htm
The different kinds of grasslands.
(Missouri Botanical Garden)

www.tallgrass.org
Tallgrass prairies.
(Neal Smith National Wildlife Refuge)

Index

ambush bug, 28, 40
American goldfinch, 40

bee, 25, 43–44
birds, 14–18, 29–32, 40–41, 43, 44, 45, 46
black–eyed Susan, 26–27, 41
bobolink, 29, 41
bug, 28, 29, 40
burrow, 12, 36
butterflies, 19–21, 27, 43, 46

coltsfoot, 8
cottontail rabbit, 35, 42
crab spiders, 10, 42

daisies, 8
dandelions, 6–7, 42
deer, 34, 46

flowers, 6, 8, 19, 26–28, 41, 42
fox, 13, 44–45
fritillary, 27, 43

garden spider, 23–24, 41
garter snake, 11, 42
golden garden spider, 23–24
goldfinch, 17, 40
grasses, 22, 43, 44, 45
grasshoppers, 9, 24, 45
great spangled fritillary, 27, 43

hawk, 18
hive, 25, 43–44
honeybee, 25, 43–44

kestrel, 18, 40–41
killdeer, 14–15, 16, 44

meadow, 5–21, 44
meadow vole, 36–37, 44

nest, 15, 16, 30–31, 36, 39

oxeye daisies, 8

prairie chicken, 32–33, 43

rabbit, 35, 42
red fox, 13, 44–45

Savannah sparrow, 16, 45
short–horned grasshopper, 45
snake, 11, 42
sparrow, 16, 45
spiders, 10, 23–24, 28, 41, 42
swallowtail butterfly, 19, 46

tallgrass prairie, 22–39, 45
tiger swallowtail butterfly, 19, 46

vole, 36–37, 39, 44

warbler, 30–31, 46
web, 23–24
white–tailed deer, 34, 46
woodchuck, 12

yellow–throat warbler, 30–31, 46